PREPARING
INSTRUCTIONAL
OBJECTIVES

Robert F. Mager

FEARON PUBLISHERS
Lear Siegler, Inc., Education Division
Belmont, California

Books by Robert F. Mager

Goal Analysis

Analyzing Performance Problems
(with Peter Pipe)

Developing Attitude Toward Learning

Developing Vocational Instruction
(with Kenneth M. Beach, Jr.)

Preparing Instructional Objectives

ISBN-0-8224-5601-X

TO

DICK LEWIS, *whose constant encouragement to write this book caused me to spend many hours at work which could otherwise have been spent at play;*

JEANNE, *who* really *understands;*

TED HUNTER, *as a small down payment on a large debt;*

ED HEROLD, *who will be surprised to hear of the existence of this work;*

OLGA SKLORD, *who will never hear of the existence of this work; and*

NORLA HIRSUTE, *who doesn't exist at all.*

FOREWORD

Everybody talks about defining educational objectives, but almost nobody does anything about it. Books on education often stress objectives; "how-to" papers on programming list "defining objectives" as a first point; and training materials such as films and filmstrips often contain a description of the "objectives." But how often are educational units, whether large or small, prepared in response to the questions:

1. What is it that we must teach?
2. How will we know when we have taught it?
3. What materials and procedures will work best to teach what we wish to teach?

Not only must these questions be answered to instruct effectively, but the order in which they are answered is important. The first question must be answered before the other two.

The probable reason that objectives are usually stated poorly is that few people know how to proceed. This is not surprising, because little has been written on the preparation of objectives—*very* little for the schoolteacher. And with the all-important business of teaching occupying their capacities, it is easy for schoolteachers to feel that they have their objectives well "in mind," and that it is neither necessary nor possible to be more specific.

Preparing Instructional Objectives makes a start toward describing how to specify objectives. It is not intended to be the last word on the subject. Rather, it is something like the first word. But the quantum jump of progress is large and real. Not only does the book provide a valuable approach to the task of goal-specification, it also supplies an *orientation* that views goal-specification as an unavoidable, practical problem requiring hard-headed solutions. This is an important step, since the proof of any method pudding is in the criterion eating.

Robert Mager has seen the need for specific instruction on the statement of objectives, and he has done something about it. The success of his efforts will be determined in part by how well you do on the criterion test that is included in the book. However, the ultimate value of the book will depend upon how much you are inspired to communicate *your own* instructional objectives.

JOHN B. GILPIN
Research Associate
Self-instruction Project
Earlham College
Richmond, Indiana

PREFACE

Once upon a time a Sea Horse gathered up his seven pieces of eight and cantered out to find his fortune. Before he had traveled very far he met an Eel, who said,

"Psst. Hey, bud. Where 'ya goin'?"

"I'm going out to find my fortune," replied the Sea Horse, proudly.

"You're in luck," said the Eel. "For four pieces of eight you can have this speedy flipper, and then you'll be able to get there a lot faster."

"Gee, that's swell," said the Sea Horse, and paid the money and put on the flipper and slithered off at twice the speed. Soon he came upon a Sponge, who said,

"Psst. Hey, bud. Where 'ya goin'?"

"I'm going out to find my fortune," replied the Sea Horse.

"You're in luck," said the Sponge. "For a small fee I will let you have this jet-propelled scooter so that you will be able to travel a lot faster."

So the Sea Horse bought the scooter with his remaining money and went zooming through the sea five times as fast. Soon he came upon a Shark, who said,

"Psst. Hey, bud. Where 'ya goin'?"

"I'm going out to find my fortune," replied the Sea Horse.

"You're in luck. If you'll take this short cut," said the Shark, pointing to his open mouth, "you'll save yourself a lot of time."

"Gee, thanks," said the Sea Horse, and zoomed off into the interior of the Shark, there to be devoured.

The moral of this fable is that if you're not sure where you're going, you're liable to end up someplace else—and not even know it.

Before you prepare instruction, before you choose material, machine, or method, it is important to be able to state clearly what your goals are. This book is about instructional objectives. In it I will try to show how to state objectives that best succeed in communicating your intent to others. The book is NOT about the philosophy of education, nor is it about *who* should select objectives, nor about *which* objectives should be selected.

It is assumed that you are interested in preparing effective instruction, and that you have taught, are teaching, or are learning to teach. It is further assumed that you are interested in communicating certain skills and knowledge to your students, and in communicating them in such a way that your students will be able to *demonstrate* their achievement of *your* instructional objectives. (If you are *not* interested in demonstrating achievement of your objectives, you have just finished this book.)

Palo Alto, California
November, 1961

ROBERT F. MAGER

CONTENTS

Occasionally you will find material presented on a left-hand page of this book. This is auxiliary material that you may find interesting, informative, or useful, but which is not essential to your reaching the objectives stated in this book.

NOTE

Much of this book has been put together differently from most books you have read. On many of the pages you will be asked a question. When this happens, select the best answer and then turn to the page number given beside that answer. In this way, the material will be adjusted to your needs and you can proceed without being distracted by unnecessary explanations.

Because the pages of this book are not read consecutively, it would be helpful to use a bookmark to help you to keep your place.

TURN TO PAGE 1.

This book is not concerned with which objectives are desirable or good. It concerns itself with the form of a usefully stated objective, rather than with its selection. The purpose of this book is limited to helping you specify and communicate those educational intents you have selected.

1

OBJECTIVES

Once an instructor decides he will teach his students something, several kinds of activity are necessary on his part if he is to succeed. He must first decide upon the goals he intends to reach at the end of his course or program. He must then select procedures, content, and methods that are relevant to the objectives; cause the student to interact with appropriate subject matter in accordance with principles of learning; and, finally, measure or *evaluate* the student's performance *according to the objectives or goals* originally selected.

The first of these, the description of objectives, is the theme of this discussion. If you are interested in preparing instruction that will help you reach your objectives, you must first be sure your objectives are clearly and unequivocally stated. You cannot concern yourself with the problem of selecting the most efficient route to your destination until you know what your destination is.

Specifically, the objectives of this book are such that, if they are achieved, you will be able to perform the following tasks:

1. Given one or more instructional objectives, you will be able to select those stated in performance terms.
2. Given a well-written instructional objective, you will be able to identify the portion of it that defines minimum acceptable performance.
3. Given one or more performance (test) items, you will be able to select those appropriate to the evaluation of the objectives.

Why "To *know* how to write objectives" has not been listed as one of the objectives of the book will become clear by the time you have read much further.

To help reach these goals, I will describe some of the advantages to be gained from the careful specification of teaching objectives, describe the characteristics of usefully stated objectives, provide some practice in recognizing well-stated goals, provide practice in selecting test items appropriate to the evaluation of an objective, and, finally, provide you with an opportunity to see just how well I have succeeded.

> *Occasionally you will find material presented on a left-hand page of this book. This is auxiliary material that you may find interesting, informative, or useful, but which is not essential to your reaching the objectives stated above.*

Three of the terms that will be used bear defining:

Behavior................refers to any visible activity displayed by a learner (student).

Terminal behavior......refers to the behavior you would like your learner to be able to demonstrate at the time your influence over him ends.

Criterion................is a standard or test by which terminal behavior is evaluated.

Throughout the book, the words "instructor" and "programmer" will be used interchangeably, as there is no difference between the classroom and the auto-instructional program in the *importance* of specifying objectives.

TURN TO PAGE 3.

Here is an example of how, without careful statements of objectives, activities in the classroom can hinder the student in his efforts to achieve an objective.

At a large training establishment operated by the government, a course was once offered in which students were to learn how to operate and repair a large, complex electronic system. The objective of the course was simply stated: To be able to operate and maintain the XYZ Electronic System.

Since it was impossible to provide each student with a separate system on which to practice (because of the exorbitant cost), it was decided to increase the amount of troubleshooting the student did during the course by giving him some "practice" in the classroom as well as in the laboratory.

During the classroom troubleshooting exercises, the instructor would pose various problems for his students to solve. He would point out a component on one of the many schematic diagrams of the equipment and ask, "What would happen if this tube were bad?" Students would then trace through the circuitry (on paper) in an effort to divine the symptoms that would appear as a result of the instructor's hypothetical trouble. The students were given a trouble and asked to induce symptoms.

This procedure, however, was exactly opposite *to that which was expected of the learner on the final examination or on the job.* There *he was typically shown a* symptom *and asked to locate the* trouble. *The instructors were expecting the learner to run forward by teaching him how to run backward.*

Thus, for want of a specific statement of objectives, students were not only learning the wrong thing, but the habits they were developing in the classroom were in conflict with those they were expected to use on the job.

2

WHY WE CARE
ABOUT OBJECTIVES

An objective is an *intent* communicated by a statement describing a proposed change in a learner—a statement of what the learner is to be like when he has successfully completed a learning experience. It is a description of a pattern of behavior (performance) we want the learner to be able to demonstrate. As Dr. Paul Whitmore once put it, "The statement of objectives of a training program must denote *measurable* attributes *observable* in the graduate of the program, or otherwise it is impossible to determine whether or not the program is meeting the objectives."

When clearly defined goals are lacking, it is impossible to evaluate a course or program efficiently, and there is no sound basis for selecting appropriate materials, content, or instructional methods. After all, the machinist does not select a tool until he knows what operation he intends to perform. Neither does a composer orchestrate a score until he knows what effects he wishes to achieve. Similarly, a builder does not select his materials or specify a schedule for construction until he has his blueprints (objectives) before him. Too often, however, one hears teachers arguing the relative merits of textbooks or other aids of the classroom versus the laboratory, without ever specifying just what goal the aid or method is to assist in achieving. I cannot emphasize too strongly the point that an instructor will function in a fog of his own making until he knows just what he wants his students to be able to do at the end of the instruction.

Another important reason for stating objectives sharply relates to the evaluation of the degree to which the learner is able

A few years ago, the chief instructor of a 32-week-long military course noticed the peculiar fact that students were doing rather poorly on every third examination. Scores were low on the first exam and then considerably better on the next two, low on the fourth and high on the next two, and so on. Since scores were consistently low and then high for even the brighter students, the instructor correctly concluded that this peculiarity was not due to student intelligence or to the lack of it. He then decided that he was so close to the course he probably wasn't seeing the woods for the trees and called in consultants.

During their analysis of the situation, these consultants noticed that the course was divided into five subcourses. Each subcourse was taught by a different team of instructors; and, during each subcourse, the students were given three examinations. They discovered that students did poorly on the first test because they weren't told what to expect; they had to use the first test as a means of finding out what the instructors expected. Once they had learned what the objectives were, they did much better on the next two exams of that subcourse. But then another team of instructors took over. Believing their examinations would be similar to those of the first team, the students prepared themselves accordingly, only to discover that the rules had been changed without their knowledge. They then did poorly on the fourth test (the first test given by the new instructor team). And so it went throughout the course. Objectives were vague, and the students were never told what to expect.

Once these conditions were made known to the chief instructor, the entire problem was easily solved.

to perform in the manner desired. Tests or examinations are the mileposts along the road of learning and are supposed to tell the teacher and the student the degree to which both have been successful in their achievement of the course objectives. But unless goals are clearly and firmly fixed in the minds of both parties, tests are at best misleading; at worst, they are irrelevant, unfair, or useless. To be useful they must measure *performance in terms of the goals.* Unless the programmer himself has a clear picture of his instructional intent, he will be unable to select test items that clearly reflect the student's ability to perform the desired skills, or that will reflect how well the student can demonstrate his acquisition of desired information.

An additional advantage of clearly defined objectives is that the student is provided the means to evaluate *his own* progress at any place along the route of instruction and is able to organize his efforts into relevant activities. With clear objectives in view, the student knows which activities on his part are relevant to his success, and it is no longer necessary for him to "psych out" the instructor. As you know too well, considerable time and effort are frequently spent by students in learning the idiosyncrasies of their teachers; and, unfortunately, this knowledge is often very useful to the student with insight. *He* may breeze through a course armed with no more than a bag full of tricks designed to rub the teacher the right way.

Before I begin to discuss what I mean by a "meaningfully stated objective," it would be well to make sure you understand what an objective is. Look at the following statement and then answer the question below it. *Check your answer by turning to the page shown beside the answer you select.*

> A general survey of the organization and administration of elementary and secondary school libraries with emphasis on methods of developing the library as an integral part of the school. Includes functions, organization, services, equipment, and materials. ﹅

What does the statement above represent? Does the statement look more like an *objective* of a course, or does it look more like a *description* of a course?

An objective of a course..*turn to page 6.*

A description of a course..*turn to page 9.*

Ooops! You didn't follow instructions. Nowhere in this book are you directed to this page. When you are asked a question, you are to select what you think is the correct or appropriate alternative and turn to the page indicated beside that alternative.

You see, I am trying to tailor my comments to your needs by asking you to answer some questions as you go. In this way, it will not be necessary to bore you with additional explanations when a single one will do.

So go back to the previous page and read the instructions again.

You said the statement was an objective of a course. Apparently I didn't make myself clear earlier, so let me try again.

A course *description* tells you something about the content and procedures of a course; a course *objective* describes a desired outcome of a course. Perhaps the sketch below will help make the distinction clear.

PREREQUISITES
what a learner has to be able to do to qualify for a course.

DESCRIPTION
what the course is about.

OBJECTIVES
what a successful learner is able to do at the end of the course.

Whereas an objective tells what the learner is to be like as a result of some learning experiences, the course description tells only what the course is about.

The distinction is quite important, because a course description does not explain what will be accepted as adequate achievement; it does not confide to the learner the rules of the game. Though a course description might tell the learner which field he will be playing on, it doesn't tell him where the foul lines are, where the goalposts are located, or how he will know when he has scored.

It is useful to be able to recognize the difference between an objective and a description, so try another example.

Which of the statements below looks most like an *objective*?

To be able to explain the principles for developing reading readiness in the primary grades..*turn to page 7.*

Discusses principles, techniques, and procedures in developing reading readiness in the primary grades........................*turn to page 8.*

You said "To be able to explain the principles for developing reading readiness in the primary grades" was a statement of an objective.

Welcome back! You are correct! The statement describes an *aim* rather than a course. It doesn't do a very good job of it, but at least it does attempt to describe a goal rather than a process.
Now let us move on.

TURN TO PAGE 10.

Oh, come on now! The collection of words that led you to this page is a piece of a course description, and not a very good description at that. I hope you are not being misled by the fact that college catalogs are composed of such phrases. They are *not* statements of intended learning outcomes and they are *not* what we are concerned with here.

Let me try to explain the difference this way. A course description describes various aspects of a PROCESS known as a "course." A course objective, on the other hand, is a description of a PRODUCT, of what the learner is supposed to be like as a *result* of the process.

Return to page 6 and read the material again.

If you have prepared an explicit statement of objectives for your own course, you will be in an excellent position to evaluate the appropriateness of commercially produced programs by comparing the objectives stated by the program producer with your own. If the program producer has not stated the objectives of his program, the rule should be "caution before buying," for you will have been put in the position of being asked to buy a product whose characteristics and features must be guessed at.

Surely, if programmed instruction succeeds in changing learners, it is not unreasonable to ask program producers to tell us how our learners will be changed as a result of studying the program, what the prerequisite knowledge of our learners should be, the nature of the population on which the program was developed and tested, and the nature of the population the program is intended for.

You said the statement was the description of a course. And right you are! I'm sure you recognize the statement as a course description lifted from a college catalog.

One final word about course descriptions before you move on. Though a description sometimes tells a good deal about what a course contains, it does not give the *intended outcomes* of the course. More important, it does not tell how to know when the intended outcomes have been achieved.

So, though a course description may be a perfectly legitimate item with a definite contribution to make to the scheme of things, here we are interested ONLY in course objectives.

You're doing fine, so move ahead by turning to page 10.

3

THE QUALITIES OF
MEANINGFUL OBJECTIVES

You already know that a statement of an objective describes a desired state in the learner. You also know that you have successfully achieved your objective when the learner can demonstrate his arrival at this state. But how do you write the objective to maximize the probability of your achieving it? What are the characteristics of a meaningfully stated objective?

Basically, a meaningfully stated objective is one that succeeds in communicating to the reader the writer's instructional intent. It is meaningful to the extent it conveys to others a picture (of what a successful learner will be like) identical to the picture the writer has in mind. Since a statement of an objective is a collection of words and symbols, it is clear that various combinations may be used to express a given intent. What you are searching for is that group of words and symbols that will communicate your intent exactly as YOU understand it. For example, if you provide another teacher with an objective, and he then teaches his students to perform in a manner that *you agree* is consistent with what you had in mind, then you have communicated your objective in a meaningful manner. If, on the other hand, you do not agree that these learners are able to perform according to your intentions, if you feel that you "had something more in mind" or that your intent was "misinterpreted," then your statement has failed to communicate adequately.

A meaningfully stated objective, then, is one that succeeds in communicating your intent; the best statement is the one that excludes the greatest number of possible alternatives to your goal.

Unfortunately, there are many "loaded" words, words open to a wide range of interpretation. To the extent that you use ONLY such words, you leave yourself open to *mis*interpretation.

Consider the following examples of words in this light:

WORDS OPEN TO MANY INTERPRETATIONS	WORDS OPEN TO FEWER INTERPRETATIONS
to know	to write
to understand	to recite
to *really* understand	to identify
to appreciate	to differentiate
to *fully* appreciate	to solve
to grasp the significance of	to construct
to enjoy	to list
to believe	to compare
to have faith in	to contrast

What do you mean when you say you want a learner to "know" something? Do you mean that you want him to be able to recite, to solve, or to construct? Just to tell him you want him to "know" tells him little—the word can mean many things.

Though it is all right to include such words as "understand" and "appreciate" in a statement of an objective, the statement is not explicit enough to be useful until it indicates how you intend to sample the "understanding" and "appreciating." Until you describe what the learner will be DOING when demonstrating that he "understands" or "appreciates," you have described very little at all. Thus, the statement that communicates best will be one that describes the terminal behavior of the learner well enough to preclude misinterpretation.

How can you write objectives that will describe the desired behavior of the learner? Well, there must be any number of schemes for doing so; but the method that is described on the pages that follow is one that is known to work, and it is the one that I have found to be the easiest to use.

One need not consider himself an unmitigated oaf for using such words as "appreciate" and "understand" in his statements of objectives, provided you go on to explain what you mean by them. One way to do this is to include the intended meaning in the same statement. Another is to use the term in an over-all objective intended merely to identify the appropriate subject matter, and then to write as many specific statements as are necessary to communicate the intent.

First, identify the terminal behavior by name; you can specify the kind of behavior that will be accepted as evidence that the learner has achieved the objective.

Second, try to define the desired behavior further by describing the important conditions under which the behavior will be expected to occur.

Third, specify the criteria of acceptable performance by describing how well the learner must perform to be considered acceptable.

Although each of these items might help an objective to be more specific, it will not be necessary to include all three in each objective. The object is to write objectives that communicate; the characteristics described above are merely offered as guides to help you know when you have done so. You do not work on an objective until it demonstrates these characteristics; rather, you work on it until it clearly communicates one of your intended educational outcomes—and you write as many statements as are needed to describe *all* your intended outcomes.

You can test whether a written objective clearly defines a desired outcome by answering "yes" to the following question:

Can another competent person select successful learners in terms of the objective so that you, the objective writer, agree with the selections?

The chapters that follow describe in some detail just how this can be done.

TURN TO THE NEXT PAGE.

4

IDENTIFYING THE
TERMINAL BEHAVIOR

A statement of an objective is useful to the extent that it specifies what the learner must be able to DO or PERFORM when he is demonstrating his mastery of the objective. Since no one can see into another's mind to determine what he knows, you can only determine the state of the learner's intellect or skill by observing some aspects of his behavior or performance (the term "behavior," as used here, means overt action). Now, the behavior or performance of the learner may be verbal or nonverbal. He may be asked to respond to questions verbally or in writing, to demonstrate his ability to perform a certain skill, or to solve certain kinds of problems. But whatever method is used, you (the programmer) can only infer the state or condition of his intellect through observation of his performance.

Thus, the most important characteristic of a useful objective is that it *identifies the kind of performance* that will be accepted as evidence that the learner has achieved the objective.

For example, consider the following statement of an objective:

> To develop a critical understanding of the operation of
> the Target Tracking Console.

Though this might be an important objective to reach, the statement doesn't tell what the learner will be doing when he is demonstrating that he has reached the objective. The words that come closest to describing what the programmer wants the learner to be able to DO are "critical understanding," and it is doubtful that

any two people would agree on the meaning of this term. Certainly, the term does not tell a learner how to organize his own efforts in order to reach the objective.

Here is an example of a more appropriately stated objective:

When the learner completes the program of instruction,
he must be able to identify by name each of the controls
located on the front of the Target Tracking Console.

What words tell what the learner will be doing when demonstrating his achievement of the objective? The words "identify by name." The objective communicates to the learner the kind of response that will be expected of him when his mastery of the objective is tested.

The way to write an objective that meets the first requirement, then, is to write a statement describing one of your educational intents and then modify it until it answers the question,

What is the learner DOING when he is demonstrating
that he has achieved the objective?

Let's apply this test to some examples. Which of the following objectives would you say is stated in behavioral, or performance, terms?

To develop an appreciation for music............*turn to page 15.*

To be able to solve quadratic equations.........*turn to page 16.*

15

Though I can understand how you might say that "To develop an appreciation for music" is stated in performance terms, you are *not* correct.

Let's ask the key question of this objective. What is the learner DOING when he is demonstrating that he has achieved this objective? What is he doing when he is "appreciating" music? You can surely see that, as now stated, the objective does not give the answer. Since the objective neither precludes nor defines any behavior, it would be necessary to accept *any* of the following behavior as evidence that the learner appreciates music:

1. The learner sighs in ecstasy when listening to Bach.
2. The learner buys a hi-fi system and $500 worth of records.
3. The learner correctly answers 95 multiple-choice questions on the history of music.
4. The learner writes an eloquent essay on the meanings of 37 operas.
5. The learner says, "Oh, man, this is the most. It's just *too* much."

Remember, I am not suggesting that "to develop an appreciation for music" isn't an important objective to try to achieve. The point is that with an objective stated as vaguely as this one is, no one has the slightest idea of the intent of the person who selected the objective. It may be a worthy objective, but, as stated above, it fails to communicate.

Now return to page 14 and select the other answer.

16

You said "To be able to solve quadratic equations" is an objective stated in behavioral terms.

Correct. This objective tells what the learner will be doing when he is demonstrating that he has reached the goal. He will be solving quadratic equations.

Suppose the learner could demonstrate that he could *derive* a quadratic equation. Would this kind of performance show that the student had reached the objective?

Yes, it would ....*turn to page 17.*

No, it wouldn't ....*turn to page 18.*

Suppose I offered to sell you an automobile for $500, and suppose I claimed that this auto was in "excellent condition" but refused to let you take a look at it. Would you buy it?

Suppose I offered to teach your children to be LOGICAL THINKERS for $1,000. Now, if I could do it, you would be getting a real bargain. But would you agree to such a bargain unless I told you beforehand more explicitly what I intended to accomplish and how we would measure my success? I hope not.

In a sense, a teacher makes a contract with his students. The students agree to pay a certain sum in return for certain skills and knowledge. But, most of the time, they are expected to pay for something that is never carefully defined or described. They are asked to buy (with effort) a product that they are not allowed to see and that is only vaguely described. The teacher who doesn't clearly specify his instructional objectives, who doesn't describe to the best of his ability how he intends the learner to be different after his instruction, is certainly taking unfair advantage of his students.

17

You said "Yes, it would." You think that if the learner can demonstrate that he can derive a quadratic equation, he has reached the objective. Well, let's look at the objective again and note carefully how it is stated—To be able to *solve* quadratic equations.

The statement doesn't say anything about *deriving* equations, does it? Now, if you feel that the learner *should* be able to derive a particular equation as well as solve it, then you would write another objective that defines what you mean by derive, or expand the one you have to include the desired equation-deriving skill. But as it is stated, the objective does not include deriving behavior in the activities that you could accept as evidence that the learner has satisfied the requirements of the objective.

You need not be concerned over the fact that the objective stated covers such a small proportion of the skills and knowledge you hope to impart during an entire course. You simply write an objective covering *each* class of skill or knowledge that you want the student to acquire. The more such statements you have, the better you have succeeded in communicating your educational intent.

Now return to page 16 and select the other answer.

Perhaps you have had academic experiences similar to this one. During class periods of a seventh grade algebra course, the teacher provided a good deal of skillful guidance in the solution of simple equations and made sure that each student had enough practice to give him confidence in his ability. When it came time for an examination, however, the items consisted mainly of stated (word) problems, and the students performed rather poorly. The teacher's justification for this "sleight of test" was that the students didn't "really understand" algebra if they could not solve word problems.

Perhaps the teacher was right. But the skill of solving equations is considerably different from the skill of solving word problems; if he wanted his students to learn how to solve word problems, he should have taught them how to do so.

Don't expect a learner to be able to exhibit skill B simply because you have given him practice in skill A.

18

You said that equation-*deriving* wouldn't do as evidence of competence in equation-*solving;* and if this was your first choice, you are doing fine.

Absolutely correct! The objective called for equation-*solving* behavior and did not mention deriving behavior. If you DID want to impart skill in equation-*deriving*, you should communicate this goal by writing another objective.

If you write your objective in meaningful (useful) terms, you will invariably have filled several pages by the time you have considered an entire course. The more objectives you include, the more successfully you will communicate your intent. In any case, it is not being honest with your students to tell them that you want them to learn to *solve* equations and then *test* them with questions asking them to do something entirely different. The way to avoid accidentally turning into such an academic sneak is to make your educational intents clear to *yourself* as well as to your students.

Let's try another example. Which of the following objectives is stated in performance terms?

To be able to repair a radio.............................*turn to page 19.*

To know how an amplifier works...................*turn to page 20.*

19

You said "To be able to repair a radio" is stated in behavioral terms. Good for you! This objective meets the first criterion of a useful statement, because it tells *what the learner will be doing* when demonstrating his achievement of the objective. He will be *"repairing* a radio."

Let's try just one more example. Which of the following is stated in performance terms?

To be able to write a summary of the factors leading to the depression of 1929..................*turn to page 21.*

To understand the rules of logic..................*turn to page 22.*

To know the rules of football..................*turn to page 23.*

20

You said "To know how an amplifier works" is stated in performance terms. But what will the learner be DOING when he is demonstrating that he KNOWS how an amplifier works?

Suppose I taught you about amplifiers, and to show me that you *know* how they work you draw a diagram of one. And suppose I fail you because I say that being able to draw an object doesn't mean you REALLY know how it works. Then, suppose you obtain a collection of parts and some tools and build me an amplifier that works and I fail you again because I contend that *building* an amplifier doesn't prove you REALLY know how one works either. You would surely be reaching for my throat by this time, and with good reason. But I think you get the point. There isn't anything "wrong" with the word KNOW—except that when it is used as the only explanatory term in a statement of objectives, it doesn't succeed in explaining very much. It just fails to communicate.

Now, knowing how an amplifier works can imply an ability to design one, an ability to build one, an ability to describe the purpose of each of the components used in one, etc. Each of these is a fine, upstanding objective in itself, but WHICH of them is implied by the word KNOW is not at all clear.

Return to page 18 and select the other answer.

21

You said "To be able to write a summary of the factors leading to the depression of 1929" was stated in performance terms.

Absolutely correct! Apparently you applied the key question to this objective and correctly concluded that the learner should be "writing a summary." He wouldn't be reciting a summary, or recognizing factors in a long list of factors, or even dictating a summary. The learner would know that in order to demonstrate achievement of his objective he would have to write a summary of factors of some sort.

And speaking of summaries, turn to page 24.

22

You said "To understand the rules of logic" is stated in performance terms.

Well, let's ask the key question of this statement. What will the learner be DOING when he is *understanding* the rules of logic? Will he be reciting them? Will he be listing them? Will he be solving problems in logic? If so, what kind of problems? This objective doesn't say. You must decide what you will accept as evidence of "understanding" and then describe this intent in your objective.

Return to page 19 and select another answer.

23

You said "To know the rules of football" is stated in performance terms.

Well, once again, let's ask of this statement the key question. What will the learner be DOING when he is showing that he has reached this objective? Will he be reciting rules? Will he be writing a list of rules? Will he be playing the game without breaking any of the rules? Will he be watching others play the game and pointing out errors as he sees them? The objective does not tell us.

Now return to page 19 and select another answer.

24

FIRST SUMMARY

1. An instructional objective describes an intended *outcome* rather than a description or summary of content.
2. One characteristic of a usefully stated objective is that it is stated in behavioral, or performance, terms that describe what the learner will be DOING when demonstrating his achievement of the objective.
3. The statement of objectives for an entire program of instruction will consist of several specific statements.
4. The objective that is most usefully stated is one that best communicates the instructional intent of the person selecting the objective.

TURN TO THE NEXT PAGE.

5

FURTHER DEFINING
THE TERMINAL BEHAVIOR

By the time you have written an objective that identifies the behavior you will expect your learners to exhibit when they have successfully completed your program, you will have written a far less equivocal objective than most that are in use today. Rather than expect your students to divine what you might have in mind when using such ambiguous words as "understand," "know," or "appreciate," you will have at least identified for him (and for yourself) the kind of activity that will be accepted as evidence of achievement. And more importantly, perhaps, you will have begun to specify your objectives in a manner that will allow you to select relevant content for your instruction and that will provide you with a basis for evaluating instruction prepared by others.

But simply specifying the terminal act may not be enough to prevent your being misunderstood. For example, an objective such as "to be able to run the 100-yard dash" is probably stated in enough detail to prevent serious misunderstanding. But a statement such as "to be able to compute a correlation coefficient" is another matter. Though this latter objective does name a terminal act, there are some serious shortcomings in the statement; there are several important ways in which the learner can misinterpret the intent. What kinds of correlations will the learner be expected to compute? Is it important to follow a specified *procedure*, or will only a correct *solution* be considered important? Will the learner be provided a list of formulas, or will he be expected to work

At one industrial organization, it became desirable to teach some employees "to be able to read electrical meters." Since there are several skills implied by this general statement, and since it was desired that the learner be able to use the statement of objectives as one means of evaluating his own progress, the final statement contained an objective defining each skill, as follows:

1. Given a meter scale, the learner is to be able to identify the value indicated by the position of the pointer as accurately as the construction of the meter will allow.
2. The learner is to be able to identify the value indicated by the pointer on meter scales that are linear, nonlinear, reversed, or bi-directional.
3. Given a meter with a single scale and a range switch, the learner is to be able to identify the value indicated by the pointer for each of the ranges shown by the range switch.
4. Given a meter with several scales and a range switch, the learner is to be able to identify the scale corresponding to each setting of the range switch.

I hope you will agree that with the statement of objectives above, you would have a far more accurate picture of what is expected of you than if you were provided with a statement that simply said "to be able to read electrical meters."

entirely without reference or calculating aids of any kind? The answer to each of these questions will make a rather important difference in the program's content and emphasis, in the accuracy with which the learner will be able to direct his efforts, and in the test situation that will be appropriate to the objective.

To state an objective that will successfully communicate your educational intent, you will sometimes have to define terminal behavior further by stating the conditions you will impose upon the learner when he is demonstrating his mastery of the objective. Here are some examples:

> Given a problem of the following class . . .
> Given a list of . . .
> Given any reference of the learner's choice . . .
> Given a matrix of intercorrelations . . .
> Given a standard set of tools . . .
> Given a properly functioning . . .
> Without the aid of references . . .
> Without the aid of slide rule . . .
> Without the aid of tools . . .

For example, instead of simply specifying "to be able to solve problems in algebra," we could improve the ability of the statement to communicate by wording it something like this:

> Given a linear algebraic equation with one unknown, the learner must be able to solve for the unknown without the aid of references, tables, or calculating devices.

How detailed should you be in your definition of terminal behavior? You should be detailed enough to be sure the target behavior would be recognized by another competent person, and detailed enough so that other possible behaviors would not be mistaken for the desired behavior. You should be detailed enough, in other words, so that others understand your intent as YOU understand it.

If you have been well steeped in behavior theory, you will see that what are being referred to here as "conditions" are more accurately described as behavior descriptions. Certainly, "calculating with a slide rule" is different behavior than "calculating with an adding machine." Similarly, "solving an equation" involves different behaviors when done with the aid of references than when done without the aid of references.

Though I will admit that all observable activity of an organism can be called behavior, and though I will admit the technical accuracy of a statement such as "writing with a long pencil involves different behavior than writing with a stubby pencil." I maintain that the difference hinders more than it helps insofar as the preparation of instructional objectives is concerned; for if you set out to define all aspects of the behavior you intend to develop, you would soon be caught in a quagmire of irrelevancies.

To help identify those aspects of terminal behavior worth mentioning, you should describe enough conditions for the objective to imply clearly the kind of test items appropriate for sampling the behavior you are interested in developing.

27

Here are some questions you can ask yourself about your objectives as a guide to identifying important aspects of the terminal behaviors that you wish to develop:

1. What will the learner be provided?
2. What will the learner be denied?
3. What are the conditions under which you will expect the terminal behavior to occur?
4. Are there any skills that you are specifically NOT trying to develop? Does the objective exclude such skills?

To see if I have made myself clear, look at the objective below and turn to the page indicated under the part of the sentence you think tells something about the conditions under which the terminal behavior is to occur.

Given a list of factors leading to significant historical events,

(Turn to page 28.)

the learner must be able to select at least five factors con-

(Turn to page 29.)

tributing to the depression of 1929.

28

You selected "Given a list of factors leading to significant historical events" as the words describing the conditions or situation under which the selecting behavior is to occur.

Very good! These words tell us that the learner will not be expected to select factors from a library of books, from an essay on history, or from his memory. It tells him that he will be provided a list and that he will be expected to recognize rather than recall.

Here is another example of an objective. Does it contain words describing the conditions under which the criterion behavior is to occur?

Given a list of 35 chemical elements, the learner must be able to recall and write the valences of at least 30.

Yes..*turn to page 30.*

No...*turn to page 31.*

29

You said the phrase "the learner must be able to select etc." describes conditions under which the selecting behavior would be expected to occur. Perhaps you are still thinking of the first characteristic of a useful objective, the one requiring the identification of the terminal behavior. If so, I'm glad you remembered it. But we are now asking for words that describe the situation or conditions under which terminal behavior will be evaluated. Perhaps it will help you to recognize such words in an objective if you ask the question, "*With* what or *to* what is the learner doing whatever it is he is doing?"

Return to page 27 and select the other alternative.

30

You said the statement DOES tell us something about the conditions under which the learner will be recalling the valences of elements. Correct! It tells us that he will be given a list of elements. There is another interesting feature of this objective, so let's look at it again.

> Given a list of 35 chemical elements, the learner must
> be able to recall and write the valences of at least 30.

Note that the statement also tells us something about what kind of behavior will be considered "passing." It tells us that 30 correct out of 35 is the *minimum acceptable skill.* (If you suspect that this touches on another characteristic of a clearly stated objective, you are correct again. I will have more to say about this in Chapter 6, "Stating the Criterion.")

Now proceed to page 32.

31

You thought the statement did NOT contain words describing the criterion (test) situation. Let's look at the statement again.

Given a list of 35 chemical elements, the learner must be able to recall and write the valences of at least 30.

Clearly, the statement meets the first requirement and describes what the learner will be doing when he demonstrates his ability to "pass" the objective; he will be *writing the valences of various elements*. Does the statement also tell anything about the references the student will be allowed to use or the materials he will be given to work with while he is doing his recalling? It *does*, doesn't it? It says that the student will be given a list of elements from which to work.

Return to page 28 and select the correct answer.

32

Very often, a good way to explain to the learner the conditions under which he will be expected to perform is simply to show him some sample test items. Many teachers make it a practice to show students at least a page of sample test items at the very beginning of a course in order that the students have a clear picture of the conditions under which they will be evaluated.

When test items are used as part of the goal statement, one of several approaches may be used. One might state, for example, that:

> The learner must be able to solve the following type of equation:
> $$Ax^2 + Bx + C = 0$$

or:

> The student must demonstrate his comprehension of the legal powers of the state over the curriculum by being able to answer correctly questions of the following type:
>
> > Following is a detailed schedule of activities included in a single day at a hypothetical elementary school. Indicate which of these activities are illegal according to the laws of the state, and add activities that are called for by state laws but which are not included in the schedule. (Schedule of activities inserted here.)

or that:

> The student must be able to demonstrate his understanding of the rules of logic by correctly solving problems of the following type:
>
> > Which of the following statements is illustrated by the Venn diagram below:
> >
> > 1. All animals are birds.
> > 2. Some birds are animals.
> > 3. All birds are animals.
> > 4. No birds are animals.

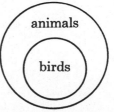

33

Regardless of how you choose to present it, your statement of objective will define the behavior more sharply if it contains words describing the situation (givens, allowances, restrictions) under which the student will be expected to show his achievement of the objective.

Before summarizing this chapter and moving on to the last guide for preparing useful objectives, here is a method for testing the clarity with which an objective describes the desired terminal behavior.

Given an objective and a set of test items or situations, *accept or reject* each test item on the basis of whether the objective defines (includes) the behavior asked for. (This procedure is analogous to analyzing a contract to see which situations are "covered" by the contract and which are not.) If you must accept all kinds of test items as appropriate, the objective needs to be more specific. If the objective allows you to accept those items you intend to use and allows you to reject those items you do not consider relevant or appropriate, the objective is stated clearly enough to be useful.

To illustrate this procedure, I will provide you with an objective and some test items. You pick out the test item that is appropriate to the objective—which must be considered *fair* because it represents the intent described by the objective.

Here's the objective:

When asked a question in French, the student must be able to demonstrate his understanding of the question by replying, in French, with an appropriate sentence.

Now, which of the following test situations would be appropriate to the objective?

Translate the following French sentences......*turn to page 34.*

Translate the following French questions......*turn to page 35.*

Reply, in French, to the following questions.. *turn to page 36.*

34

You chose "Translate the following French sentences." Perhaps I wasn't clear on what you are to try to do. You are to try to identify those test items or test situations that are relevant to an objective and that will tell something about whether a student has actually reached the objective you have stated. If you are clear about what you are now doing and still selected this page, then you are incorrect. The objective clearly defines the situation that will be acceptable as evidence of "understanding," and that situation is not one in which the student *translates*.

Return to page 33 and take a close look at the objective before selecting another answer.

35

You think that translating French questions into English will tell whether a student can reply to a French question IN FRENCH? Come on, now! This test item is *not* appropriate to the objective as stated. The objective clearly specifies the kind of behavior that will demonstrate the learner's competence, and it isn't *translating* behavior.

Return to page 33 and read the objective more carefully before selecting another answer.

36

You said the item "Reply, in French, to the following questions" is one that would help to measure how well the student has reached the stated objective.

Right! Absolutely right. The objective clearly stated that "understanding" would be demonstrated when the student responded, in French, to questions posed in the same language.

Now try this objective:

To be able to solve a simple linear equation.

Which of the following test items is relevant to this objective?

Solve for X in the following:
$2 + 4X = 12$ ....*turn to page 37.*

If seven hammers cost seven dollars, how much does one hammer cost? ....*turn to page 38.*

37

EXCELLENT! You saw the only way to find out whether a student has learned how to *solve* equations is to ask him to solve some equations.

Now let's look at what happens when you apply this procedure to a *poorly* stated objective. Here is the objective:

To develop a knowledge of American history.

And the question is this: Can any of the test items below be considered *inappropriate* for measuring whether a learner has reached the objective?

1. Discuss the meaning of any three significant events in American history.
2. List the names of the generals who commanded American troops during the Spanish-American War, the Civil War, and the War of Independence.
3. List as many events as you can that occurred in American history between 1850 and 1950 and give the date of each event.

Yes..*turn to page 39.*

No..*turn to page 42.*

38

Well, if you missed THIS one, and you did, I'd better sign up for some couch time. I talked about this very item earlier in this discussion, but I certainly couldn't have explained it very well if you forgot so soon.

If you expect a student to learn how to solve *word problems*, then TEACH him how to solve word problems. Do not expect him to learn to solve *word problems* by teaching him how to solve *equations*. This is like expecting a man to learn how to play a piano by teaching him how to play a trombone. Of course there are some elements common to both skills, but *NOT ENOUGH* to insure that by learning one he will automatically learn the other.

Our objective clearly stated that we wanted to teach our students to be able to SOLVE EQUATIONS. Therefore, the only appropriate way to test to see whether they have learned to *solve* equations is to ask them to *solve equations*. It is *not* appropriate to ask them to describe equations, or write essays about equations, or to solve word problems.

Return to page 33.

39

You said that one or more of the test items on page 37 are inappropriate for testing knowledge of American history. Let me ask you this. Did the objective tell you what to look for when the learner was demonstrating that he "knew" American history? Unless it did, how can you say that ANY behavior is inappropriate?

Let's try this one before we move on.

> Given a DC motor of ten horsepower or less that contains a single malfunction, and given a standard kit of tools and references, the learner must be able to repair the motor within a period of 45 minutes.

If to test whether you had reached this objective I gave you a motor with a trouble in it and then asked you only to *locate the trouble*, would my test item be appropriate to the objective?

Yes, I think it is..*turn to page 40.*

No, it is not..*turn to page 41.*

40

You said that to test an objective that asks for *repairing* behavior we can ask for *locating* behavior.

Let's look at the objective again. It said:

Given a DC motor of ten horsepower or less that contains a single malfunction, and given a standard kit of tools and references, the learner must be able to repair the motor within a period of 45 minutes.

Now, "repair the motor" means to make it work. So MAKING IT WORK is the behavior desired. The test item, however, only asked the learner to "locate" a malfunction. Therefore, the test item sampled only a portion of the behavior called for by the objective. If this test item is intended to measure the behavior stated in the objective, it is clearly inadequate. For this item to be considered appropriate, there would have to be additional test items to test for the remaining aspects of the objective.

Return to page 39 and read the material again. Then select the correct answer.

41

You said the test item is NOT appropriate to the objective. Correct! The objective asked for *repairing behavior* rather than *locating* behavior, and for me to ask for one of these after telling you I wanted you to develop skill in the other is quite unfair. Had the objective NOT been as specific as it was, you wouldn't have known exactly what you were to learn and you might have wasted much of your time, in the absence of specific information, rummaging around to discover what kind of test I gave, what my pet peeves were, and other clues to how to pass.

When you are preparing instructional content in the *absence* of specific objectives, you might neglect to provide information and practice in the very skills you are most interested in developing. You might even fall into the trap of equating the difficulty of teaching a concept with the importance of the concept.

Now go back to page 37 and see if you can answer the item correctly.

42

Very good! You saw that any of the items would have to be considered fair, or acceptable, or appropriate, according to the way the objective was stated.

The procedure, then, of evaluating test items on the basis of their appropriateness to an objective is a useful one in testing the sharpness of the objective itself. If the objective is stated in such a way as to include all the possible test situations covering the subject, then it is too vaguely stated to communicate much of your intent to the learner. If, on the other hand, it is stated in a manner that includes test situations you intend to use and that excludes those you feel are irrelevant, then the objective is probably stated in a clear enough manner to communicate your intent.

TURN TO THE NEXT PAGE.

43

SECOND SUMMARY

1. An instructional objective is a statement that describes an intended outcome of instruction.
2. An objective is meaningful to the extent it communicates an instructional intent to its reader, and does so to the degree that it describes or defines the terminal behavior expected of the learner.
3. Terminal behavior is defined by:
   a. Identifying and naming the observable act that will be accepted as evidence that the learner has achieved the objective.
   b. Describing the conditions (givens, restrictions) necessary to exclude acts that will not be accepted as evidence that the learner has achieved the objective.

TURN TO THE NEXT PAGE.

6

STATING THE CRITERION

Now that you have described what it is you want the learner to be able to do, you can increase the ability of an objective to communicate by telling the learner HOW WELL you want him to be able to do it. You will accomplish this by describing the criterion of acceptable performance.

If you can specify at least the minimum acceptable performance for each objective, you will have a performance standard against which to test your instructional programs; you will have a means for determining whether your programs are successful in achieving your instructional intent. What you must try to do, then, is indicate in your statement of objectives what the acceptable performance will be, by adding words that describe the criterion of success.

Indicate the statement that best describes your attitude at this time.

Show me how to describe minimum acceptable performance..*turn to page 45.*

Many of the things I teach are intangible and cannot be evaluated..............................*turn to page 47.*

45

All right, let's look at some of the ways in which minimum acceptable performance can be specified in your statement of objectives.

Probably the most obvious way to indicate a lower limit of acceptable performance is to specify a *time limit* where one is appropriate. This is often done informally when the learner is told how much time he will be allowed to complete an examination. When the instructor is *not* concerned about a time limit, the student is sometimes informed that he will be expected to pass a "power" test and is then given all the time he wants or needs. When you DO want to insist that the performance of the student must occur within a specified amount of time, it is only fair that you communicate this intended criterion to the learner. Consider, for example, this objective:

To be able to run the 100-yard dash.

If you do NOT intend to evaluate the learner on the basis of the speed with which he runs, you need not indicate a time limit. If, on the other hand, you will not consider him to have reached the objective unless he can run the distance within 14 seconds, it is only fair to let the learner in on this intent, and say:

To be able to run the 100-yard dash within a period of 14 seconds.

If, for example, you are teaching mathematics and expect your students to develop a certain amount of problem-solving proficiency, you might use the words italicized below in your objective:

The student must be able to correctly solve *at least seven* simple linear equations *within a period of thirty minutes.*

If you were interested only in having the student "understand" how to solve these equations and didn't care whether he develops any problem-solving speed, you wouldn't need to indicate a time limit. Let's look at another example in more detail.

One of the things a student TV repairman has to learn to do is to adjust a little magnet called an "ion trap," which is located on the neck of the TV picture tube. When this little magnet is in the wrong place, there will be black shadows across the face of the

tube; when it is properly placed, the face of the picture tube will be evenly lighted. The instructional objective describing the skill might be stated as follows:

> Given an otherwise properly functioning TV receiver of the following models (list of appropriate models inserted here), the learner must be able to adjust the ion trap.

Does this statement describe or indicate the criterion of acceptable performance? Does it have words that tell when the learner will be judged to have achieved the objective?

Yes..*turn to page 48.*

No..*turn to page 49.*

47

Well, all right . . . but if you are teaching skills that cannot be evaluated, you are in the awkward position of being unable to demonstrate that you are teaching anything at all.

Although it is true, in general, that the more important an objective is the more difficult it is to state, you can go a long way toward stating objectives a good deal better than has been the case up to now. And I'm convinced you will soon be able to do better than you can now. Every time you travel even a little distance toward adequate specification of an objective, you reap all the advantages and avoid all the pitfalls that have been pointed out in this book.

So let's see how far you *can* go, even though you won't be able to do as well as you would like, even by the day after tomorrow.

Go directly to page 45.

48

You said the statement describes or indicates the criterion of acceptable performance. Well, in a way you are right. Certainly the statement tells what the learner would be doing when demonstrating that he had reached the objective (adjusting an ion trap), and it tells that he would be given a properly operating set of a certain kind on which to do his adjusting. And by OMISSION, it tells that ANY kind of ion-trap adjusting behavior would be considered satisfactory. Since no limits were set on performance, you would have to accept anything the learner exhibits in the way of adjusting behavior as acceptable.

Return to page 46 and select the other alternative.

49

Correct! You saw that the statement did not describe or indicate a criterion of acceptable performance.

There are at least two ways in which this objective can be improved. The first way is to include words describing what the TV receiver will look like when the adjustment has been performed properly. The second way is to include words that define the time limit within which the adjusting must occur. If you add these improvements to the objective, it will look like this:

> Given an otherwise properly functioning TV receiver of any of the following models (insert list of appropriate models), the learner must be able to adjust the ion trap to achieve a uniform raster within a period of five minutes.
>
> (Note: "Raster" is the term used to describe a lighted but pictureless TV screen.)

One of the ways of defining acceptable performance, then, is by indicating a time limit—whenever a time limit is intended.

Another way to indicate a criterion of successful performance is to specify the *minimum* number of correct responses you will accept, the *number* of principles that must be applied in a given situation, the *number* of principles that must be identified, or the *number* of words that must be spelled correctly. For example:

> Given a human skeleton, the student must be able to correctly identify by labeling at least 40 of the following bones; there will be no penalty for guessing (list of bones inserted here).

The *minimum acceptable skill* is specified in terms of the number of bones to be identified. The student must be able to correctly identify at least 40 items, and he is encouraged to guess. There is another interesting feature of this objective that should answer one of the questions that has probably been bothering you in this chapter—how can you indicate precisely what your evaluation criteria are *without* also insisting that each learner perform in exactly the same way as every other learner? The answer can be

There is no reason why a statement of a single objective must be contained in a single sentence; to the contrary, you will find several occasions where quite a few sentences might be required to clearly communicate your intent. This is generally true, for example, where you are describing objectives requiring synthesis behavior or creative activity on the part of the learner. Here is one such example:

The student must be able to write a musical composition with a single tonal base. The composition must be at least 16 bars in length and contain at least 24 notes. The student must demonstrate his understanding of the rules of good composition by applying at least three of them in the development of his score. The student is to complete his composition within four hours.

Here is another example, this one from a human relations course:

The student is to be able to prepare an analysis of any five of the ten case studies given him at the time of examination. These analyses should attempt to discuss the cases according to the priniples developed during the course, and the student must show evidence of having considered each problem from at least two of the participants' points of view by restating these in his own words. References and notes may be used, and up to 24 hours may be taken for the writing of the five analyses.

seen in the objective statement given. Each and every learner must correctly identify *at least 40* of the skeleton's bones. The lower limit of acceptable performance is specified, but each learner can surpass that limit by performing differently than every other learner.

An alternative to indicating *number* is to indicate *percentage* or *proportion*. Thus, if appropriate, you could indicate that:

> The student must be able to reply in grammatically correct French to 95% of the French questions that are put to him during an examination.

Or you could specify:

> The student must be able to spell correctly at least 80% of the words called out to him during an examination period.

Or you could specify:

> The student must be able to write the names and addresses of at least three-fifths of the five New York doctors who recommend the ingredients in Brand X.

Another way of describing criterion behavior is that of defining the important characteristics of performance accuracy. The example about adjusting ion traps in TV receivers said that the adjusting would be considered satisfactory when the learner had achieved a "uniform raster." Now in *this* case it isn't too important if there is some discrepancy between what different persons might understand "uniform raster" to mean. The set will work just as well if there is a little shading here or there on the face of the screen. But there *are* instances where more precise performance is important to achieve, and then it *is* important to define the quality of acceptable performance in more detail.

For example, one of the skills a missile maintenance man must develop has to do with the adjustment of a round TV screen called a PPI. On the face of this screen there is a range marker that is electronically produced; one of the jobs of the maintenance man is to adjust this marker until it is *round*. But what is

For further information about objectives, you will find the following books extremely informative:

Taxonomy of Educational Objectives
Handbook I: Cognitive Domain
Benjamin S. Bloom, Editor.
New York: David McKay, Inc., 1956.

Taxonomy of Educational Objectives
Handbook II: Affective Domain
D. R. Krathwohl, B. S. Bloom, and B. B. Masia
New York: David McKay, Inc., 1964.

These books discuss the different kinds of objectives you can select and provide a good many examples of test situations appropriate for each.

It is not always possible to specify a criterion with as much detail as you would like, but this should not prevent you from trying to communicate as fully as possible with the learner and with each other. But certainly you should be able to find some way to evaluate anything you think important enough to spend a significant amount of time teaching. If you find something you feel sure you cannot measure, the place to put effort is in trying to develop some way to measure it.

round enough? How do we tell the learner how excellent he must be before we will consider him satisfactory?

Well, in this case it is important that the marker be *very round*. But by now you see quite clearly that the words "very round" do not succeed in communicating much, so you must search for a better way of describing your intent with respect to the quality of the performance you seek. One way of doing this would be to define the amount of *acceptable deviation* from some standard. You could put a round standard template on the screen and tell the learner that his marker will be "round enough" when no part of it deviates more than one-eighth inch from the standard. The objective might look something like this:

> Given a properly operating XX-1 radar system and a standard kit of tools, the learner must be able to adjust the range marker of the PPI to acceptable roundness within a period of 45 seconds. Acceptable roundness is defined as a deviation of one-eighth inch or less from a standard template.

Perhaps more familiar examples of ways in which performance accuracy is sometimes specified are these:

> ... and to be considered correct, problem solutions must be accurate to the nearest whole number.

or

> ... The student must be able to use the chemical balance well enough to weigh materials accurately to the nearest milligram.

or

> ... and when calculating with the C and D scales of the slide rule, calculations must be accurate to at least three significant figures.

As you try to write objectives that meet the requirements discussed in this book, you will undoubtedly find other ways of specifying the excellence of performance you intend to accept as evidence of the learner's success. One good way to get started is to look over the examinations you use; they will tell you what

you ARE using as standards of performance, and you can improve your objectives by putting these standards into words. Once this is done, you can ask these questions of your statements to test their clarity and completeness:

1. Does the statement describe what the learner will be doing when he is demonstrating that he has reached the objective?
2. Does the statement describe the important conditions (givens or restrictions, or both) under which the learner will be expected to demonstrate his competence?
3. Does the statement indicate how the learner will be evaluated? Does it describe at least the lower limit of acceptable performance?

If you should find yourself occasionally unable to decide whether a phrase you have written should be called a restriction or a criterion, ask yourself if the phrase says anything about the excellence of performance that will be expected of the student. If it does, call it a criterion. If you are still unsure what to call it, keep calm. After all, the important matter is not the label you give it, but how well it performs the function for which it is intended.

A final comment before the final summary. To familiarize you with a strategy for preparing objectives, only examples of content objectives have been used. But, of course, you frequently intend to reach objectives other than those relating merely to the content or subject matter. Where, for example, it is intended that the learner develop a certain amount of "confidence" in his handling of the subject matter, or if he is expected to acquire certain "critical attitudes," it is appropriate to decide what you will accept as evidence of "confidence" or of "critical attitudes" and describe these behaviors in separate objectives. Statements of objectives should include *all intended* outcomes, whether related to content or not; only when this is accomplished will you have a sound basis for selecting the learning experiences to include in an instructional program.

Once armed with objectives that communicate and an intent to demonstrate their achievement, you are ready to accomplish the next step in instructional design—that of preparing your criterion examination.

TURN TO THE NEXT PAGE.

53

FINAL SUMMARY

1. A statement of instructional objectives is a collection of words or symbols describing one of your educational *intents*.

2. An objective will communicate your intent to the degree you have described what the learner will be DOING when demonstrating his achievement and how you will know when he is doing it.

3. To describe terminal behavior (what the learner will be DOING):

   a. Identify and name the over-all behavior act.

   b. Define the important conditions under which the behavior is to occur (givens or restrictions, or both).

   c. Define the criterion of acceptable performance.

4. Write a separate statement for each objective; the more statements you have, the better chance you have of making clear your intent.

5. If you give each learner a copy of your objectives, you may not have to do much else.

TURN TO THE NEXT PAGE.

7

SELF-TEST

On the pages that follow, you will find a short self-test by which you can check to see how expert you are in determining whether given objectives exhibit the characteristics discussed in this book. Answer all the questions and then look at the correct answers on page 60.

For the author to have reached his objectives (stated on page 1), you can make only 7 errors, at most, out of the 44 items.

1. Are the objectives below stated in at least performance (behavioral) terms? Does each at least name an act the learner would be performing when demonstrating that he has achieved the objective?

	YES	NO
a. To understand the principles of salesmanship.	____	____
b. To be able to write three examples of the logical fallacy of the undistributed middle.	____	____
c. To be able to understand the meaning of Ohm's Law.	____	____
d. To be able to name the bones of the body.	____	____
e. To be able to list the principles of secondary school administration.	____	____
f. To know the plays of Shakespeare.	____	____
g. To *really* understand the law of magnetism.	____	____
h. To be able to identify instructional objectives that indicate what the learner will be doing when demonstrating achievement of the objective.		

2. Given below are two characteristics of a statement of instructional objectives.

   A. Identifies the behavior to be demonstrated by the student.

   B. Indicates a standard or criterion of acceptable performance.

Are each of these characteristics present in each of the objectives below? For each objective below, check whether *each* of these characteristics is present.

                                      A   B

a. The student must be able to understand the theory of evolution. Evidence of understanding will be obtained from a written essay on evolution.   ____ ____

b. The student is to be able to complete a 100-item multiple-choice examination on the subject of marine biology. The lower limit of acceptable performance will be 85 items answered correctly within an examination period of 90 minutes.   ____ ____

c. The student must be able to correctly name each item depicted by *each* of a series of 20 blueprints.   ____ ____

d. To demonstrate his ability to read an assembly blueprint, the student must be able to make the item depicted by the blueprint given him at the time of examination. Student will be allowed the use of all tools in the shop.   ____ ____

e. During the final examination, and without reference, the student must be able to write a description of the steps involved in making a blueprint.   ____ ____

f. The student is to be able to draw his service revolver and fire five rounds (shots) from the hip within a period of three

A B

seconds. At 25 yards all rounds must hit the standard silhouette target; at 50 yards he must hit with at least two of his five rounds. ____ ____

g. The student must know *well* the five cardinal rules of homicide investigation. ____ ____

h. The student must be able to fill out a standard accident report. ____ ____

i. The student must be able to write a coherent essay on the subject "How To Write Objectives for a Course in Law Appreciation." Student may use all references noted during the course, as well as class notes. Student must write his essay on paper provided by the examiner. ____ ____

j. Beside each of the following psychological principles, the student must be able to write the name of the authors of experiments on which the principle is based (list of principles appended). ____ ____

k. Given a list of objectives, the learner should be able to evaluate each. ____ ____

l. To list the important characteristics of branching and linear self-instructional programs. ____ ____

m. The student is to be able to name and give an example of each of six programming techniques useful for eliciting a correct response. To be considered correct, items listed by the student must appear on the handout entitled "Programming Techniques" issued by the instructor during the course. ____ ____

n. To develop logical approaches in the solution of personnel problems. ____ ____

3. Here is a rather poorly stated objective:

> The student must be able to understand the laws pertaining to contracts.

Indicate whether the following test situations would have to be considered appropriate for testing whether the objective had been achieved.

Test Situations	APPROPRIATE	NOT APPROPRIATE
a. The learner is asked to write the name of each of the justices of the Supreme Court.	_____	_____
b. Given a contract with certain legal terms circled, the student is asked to write a definition of each of the circled terms.	_____	_____
c. Given a legal contract and a list of contract laws, the learner is asked to indicate which of the laws, if any, are violated by the wording of the contract.	_____	_____
d. The student is asked to answer 50 multiple-choice questions on the subject of legal contracts.	_____	_____

4. Which of the test situations below would be appropriate for eliciting the kind of behavior by which you could tell if the student had reached the objective?

Objective: Given a properly functioning audiometer of any model, the student must be able to make the adjustments and control settings necessary prior to the conduct of a standard hearing test.

Test Situations	APPROPRIATE	NOT APPROPRIATE
a. List the steps, in their proper order, for setting up an audiometer for use.	_____	_____
b. Proceed to the audiometer on Table No. 5 and set it up so that it can be used to administer a standard hearing test.	_____	_____
c. Describe the steps followed in the conduct of a standard hearing test.	_____	_____
d. Discuss the role of the audiometer in the hearing clinic.	_____	_____

TURN TO PAGE 60.

60

ANSWERS TO SELF-TEST

1. a. No
    b. Yes
    c. No
    d. Yes
    e. Yes
    f. No
    g. No
    h. Yes

3. a. Not appropriate
    b. Appropriate
    c. Appropriate
    d. Appropriate

4. a. Not appropriate
    b. Appropriate
    c. Not appropriate
    d. Not appropriate

2.

	A	B
a.	Yes	No
b.	Yes	Yes
c.	Yes	Yes
d.	Yes	No
e.	Yes	No
f.	Yes	Yes
g.	No	No
h.	Yes	No
i.	Yes	No
j.	Yes	No
k.	No	No
l.	Yes	No
m.	Yes	Yes
n.	No	No

How well did you do?

Seven errors or less..*the end.*

More than seven errors.........................*go back to page 10.*